A Century
of Stories
New Hanover County Public Library
1906-2006

POWER SKATEBOARDING™

Skateboarding Half-pipes, Ramps, and Obstacles

The Rosen Publishing Group's

PowerKids Press™

New York

To Matt and Sean

Published in 2006 by The Rosen Publishing Group, Inc.
29 East 21st Street, New York, NY 10010

First Edition

Editor: Melissa Acevedo
Book Design: Elana Davidian
Photo Researcher: Jeff Wendt

Photo Credits: Cover, pp. 1, 7 (inset), 15, 16, 20 © Tony Donaldson/Icon SMI/The Rosen Publishing Group; pp. 4, 7, 12, 19 © Dan Bourqui / www.50-50.com; p. 8 (inset) © Bryce Kanights / Studio 43; pp. 8, 11 © Team Goon.

Library of Congress Cataloging-in-Publication Data

Hocking, Justin.
Skateboarding half-pipes, ramps, and obstacles / Justin Hocking.
p. cm. — (Power skateboarding)
Includes index.
ISBN 1-4042-3051-3 (library binding)
1. Skateboarding—Juvenile literature. I. Title II. Series: Hocking, Justin. Power skateboarding.

GV859.8.H6123 2006
796.22—dc22
2004026978

Manufactured in the United States of America

Contents

4 Christian Hosoi shows off his moves on a half-pipe ramp in Le Grand Bornand, France, in 1990. *Inset:* Professional skateboarder Lance Mountain skates the Animal Chin Ramp in California.

The History of Ramps and Obstacles

The first skateboard magazine was created in 1965 and was called *The Quarterly Skateboarder*. The picture on the cover shows a young Californian skater jumping over a high-jump bar balanced between two posts. This type of bar was one of the first skateboarding **obstacles**. These obstacles were like the bars that high jumpers leap over in the Olympic Games, only much lower.

Many early skateboarders were also **surfers**, who needed something to do when they could not surf. During the 1970s, they started building wooden **ramps** that curved up into the shape of a wave. These ramps are called **quarter-pipes**. The first **half-pipes** were built soon after. A half-pipe consists of two quarter-pipes that face one another and are connected in the middle by a **flat bottom**. Ramps changed skateboarding forever.

By the 1980s, skaters like Christian Hosoi and Lance Mountain were using quarter-pipes and half-pipes to reach unbelievable heights. They also used them to complete hard tricks.

With the creation of quarter-pipes and half-pipes, skaters were able to invent new tricks that would take the sport to another level. The ramps that helped elevate skateboarding to where it is today are made up of several different parts. The **transitions**, also called trannys or walls, are the curving parts of a ramp that have a wavelike shape. Transitions come in many different sizes and levels of steepness, depending on the ramp. The part called the flat bottom is the flat, ground-level part of the ramp that connects the two transitions. Most half-pipes have at least 12 feet (3.7 m) of flat bottom. This space gives skaters plenty of time to set up for tricks as they ride back and forth between transitions.

A round metal pipe, known as the **lip** or the coping, sits at the top of most ramps. The lip is a surface for doing tricks, like **grinds**. Some street-style obstacles also have lips. Most street obstacles have square instead of round lips.

This full-sized half-pipe is located in California. *Inset:* This skater is getting ready to drop in from the lip, or coping, of a half-pipe ramp.

8 The vert ramp at the YMCA Skatepark in Encinitas, California, is one of the biggest in the world. The photo above was taken at its grand opening on June 13, 2004. *Inset:* Pro skater Danny Way set a new world record in 2003 for jumping 23.5 feet (7 m) using a vert ramp.

Vert Ramps

Most modern half-pipes are **vert ramps**. Vert is short for **vertical**. They are called vert ramps because their transitions have at least 1 foot (0.3 m) that is vertical at the top. The vertical part makes vert ramps harder to ride than other ramps. However, it also allows skateboarders to jump high above the lip. Many pro vert skaters can fly as high as 12 feet (3.7 m) to 13 feet (4 m) above the lip. Most modern vert ramps are between 10 feet (3 m) and 13 feet (4 m) high. They are usually between 20 feet (6 m) and 100 feet (30 m) wide. One of the biggest vert ramps is located at the YMCA Skatepark in Encinitas, California. This vert ramp is 13 feet (4 m) high and 120 feet (37 m) long, making it one of the largest half-pipes in the world. It was originally built for a **professional** X Games contest in 2003.

Some famous Californian ramp skaters, like Tony Hawk and Bucky Lasek, use the YMCA Skatepark vert ramp in Encinitas to train for vert events around the world.

Mini Ramps

Another common type of half-pipe ramp is the **mini ramp**. Mini ramps are much shorter than vert ramps. Most mini ramps are between 4 feet (1.2 m) and 6 feet (2 m) high. Mini ramps are good for beginners when they are learning basic half-pipe skills. This is because mini ramps are smaller and less steep. Their smaller size allows professional skaters to do really hard tricks on them. Mini ramps dare pros to be more imaginative within a small skating space.

Mini ramps are also popular because they are much cheaper to build than vert ramps. They also take up much less space. For these reasons many skaters have mini ramps in their backyards. Mini ramps are also common at skate parks all across the country. The Riverside Skatepark in New York City and the Skatelab Skatepark in Simi Valley, California, are both skate parks that feature excellent mini ramps.

When building a mini ramp, it is important to consider the length and other measurements. This mini ramp was built to fit easily in a small city park.

Spines are special obstacles that connect two half-pipes at one point. A well-built spine, like the one shown above, makes an ordinary mini ramp twice as much fun.

Spines

A spine is two transitions from two half-pipes that are placed back-to-back. A spine usually has two metal lips bonded together at the top. When looked at from the side, a half-pipe with a spine looks like a huge *W*.

Spines can be different sizes, shapes, and steepnesses. They are fun to ride because they double the skating surface of a ramp. This gives skaters more room to ride and attempt different tricks. Skaters can move from one side of the ramp to the other by **transferring** over the spine. There are many ways to transfer over a spine, including with grinds. Because they are larger and more expensive, half-pipes with spines are not as common as regular half-pipes. Yet many spine ramps do exist all over the country. The Northside Aztlan Community Center in Fort Collins, Colorado, is home to what many people consider to be one of the country's best spine ramps.

Quarter-pipes and Street Obstacles

A quarter-pipe is basically one half of a half-pipe. Quarter-pipes are usually found in skate park **street courses**. A street course is part of a skate park that is made up of smaller obstacles, like **ledges** and **handrails**. These obstacles are similar to the types of obstacles you might find on a real street. Although you will not find many quarter-pipes on the street, they are an important part of a street course because they help skaters keep their speed as they move from obstacle to obstacle.

Most quarter-pipes are between 3 feet (1 m) and 10 feet (3 m) high. Some larger quarter-pipes have 1 foot (.3 m) or more of pure vertical at the top, like a vert half-pipe. Other quarter-pipes are much less steep.

The YMCA Skatepark in Encinitas, California, is home to one of the steepest quarter-pipes in the world. It is about 9 feet (2.7 m) tall and has more than 4 feet (1 m) of pure vertical.

This skater is about to do a kick flip. Kick flips are tricks in which you flip the board all the way around using your foot. *Inset:* Handrails are popular obstacles. Skaters, like the one above, use them to do daring tricks like grinds.

This skater is doing an ollie to get onto a grind box in a skate park. Grind boxes in skate parks can't be moved. Smaller grind boxes can be bought in a store, or you can build your own. A smaller grind box can be easily moved around and placed in different skate spots.

Grind Boxes

Grind boxes, also called ledges, are probably the most popular modern skate obstacles. Why are they so popular? For one thing they are really easy to move around. Grind boxes can be taken around in a car or even rolled down the street on top of a skateboard. You can also skate a grind box in a parking lot, on a sidewalk, or in a driveway. Grind boxes are also fairly cheap and easy to build.

Most grind boxes are about 2 feet (0.6 m) high and 8 feet (2.4 m) long, with a rectangular shape. They are usually made of wood, with a square metal lip, also called angle-iron, on the upper edge of the box. To get on top of the box, skaters have to **ollie**. Many different tricks can be done on a grind box, including grinds. Grind boxes are also good for doing **manuals**.

Grind boxes are among the smallest and simplest skateboard obstacles. However, hundreds of different tricks can be done on one of these boxes.

Pyramids

Just about every skate park street course includes at least one pyramid. A pyramid is an obstacle that has triangular walls, like the pyramids you might see in Egypt. Most skate park pyramids, however, have a flat top, rather than the pointy tip you see on the ancient pyramids. They are also much smaller and less steep, and they are made of wood instead of stone.

Pyramids are built with a flat top to allow skaters to do advanced tricks while gaining more speed. Most pyramids are about 3 feet (1 m) to 5 feet (1.5 m) tall. With enough speed and skill, skateboarders can ollie over the top of the pyramid and land on the opposite side. Pyramids are also perfect for tricks that are harder and require much more skill than the standard ones. Tricks such as **kick flips** are done more often on pyramids because they have flat surfaces that are easy to land on. Many pyramids also have a grind box on the top.

Skater Chris Yourgalite is doing a trick high above a pyramid in a Park City, Utah, skate park. Sometimes obstacles like handrails and ledges are added to pyramids to make tricks more challenging.

Much like grind boxes, flat bars are easy to carry around. The flat bars found in skate parks, however, cannot be moved because they are connected to the ground. This skater is doing an ollie to get onto a flat bar in a skate park.

Flat bars are another common and fun obstacle. Like grind boxes, flat bars are easy to take anywhere. Most flat bars are even lighter and easier to carry than grind boxes. They can also be skated just about anywhere. However, flat bars are harder to build than grind boxes because they are made entirely from metal. Luckily several skateboard companies sell inexpensive flat bars.

A flat bar is made of a long, flat metal bar that is supported on each end by two small beams. Most flat bars are about 1 foot (0.3 m) to 2 feet (0.6 m) high, and 6 feet (2 m) to 10 feet (3 m) long. Flat bars are good obstacles on which skaters can do tricks like grinds. To make tricks and skating more interesting, skaters can place flat bars on top of other obstacles, like half-pipes and pyramids.

A pro skateboarder named Ryan Johnson holds the current record for grinding a handrail down a set of 31 stairs. That takes some serious bravery!

Of all the skateboard obstacles, handrails are the hardest to skate. Created to make walking up and down stairs easier and safer, handrails seem like an unlikely skateboard obstacle. Yet sometime during the 1980s, a famous pro skater named Mark Gonzales decided to slide down a handrail on his skateboard. Soon skateboarders everywhere were riding handrails.

Handrails come in all shapes and sizes. The type of handrail found in skate park street courses is usually about 3 feet (1 m) high and up to 10 feet (3 m) to 12 feet (3.7 m) long. Like flat bars, handrails are also good for tricks like grinds. However, it takes an unbelievable amount of skill, balance, and daring to skate a handrail. Thanks to all the modern obstacles, skateboarding has come a long way since the days of the high jump.

Glossary

flat bottom (FLAT BAH-tum) The flat, ground-level part of the ramp that connects the two transitions.

grinds (GRYNDZ) Tricks in which you drag the trucks of your board along the lip or the top of an obstacle.

half-pipes (HAF-pyps) Ramps that are shaped like big *U*'s.

handrails (HAND-raylz) Originally created to make walking up and down stairs easier and safer, handrails are often used as obstacles in skateboarding.

kick flips (KIK FLIPS) Tricks where the side of the front foot is used to flip the board all the way around.

ledges(LEJ-ez) Small, square obstacles used for doing tricks.

lip (LIP) Also known as the coping, the lip is a round metal pipe at the top of most ramps.

manuals (MAN-yoo-ulz) Tricks in which you ride balancing only on your two back wheels.

mini ramp (MIH-nee RAMP) A common type of half-pipe ramp, mini ramps are shorter and smaller than other ramps. The standard mini ramps are between 4 feet (1.2 m) and 6 feet (2 m) high.

obstacles (OB-stih-kulz) Any objects that can be used in a skateboarding trick.

ollie (AH-lee) A special skateboarding move, or trick, in which the rider and the board lift off the ground.

professional (pruh-FEH-shuh-nul) Having to do with someone who is paid for what he or she does.

quarter-pipes (KWOR-tur-pyps) Ramps that look like half of a half-pipe.

ramps (RAMPS) Sloping platforms.

street courses (STREET KORS-ez) Skateboarding paths made up to look like the street. They have obstacles like benches, stairs, and handrails.

surfers (SERF-erz) People who use boards to ride ocean waves.

transferring (TRANS-fer-ing) Using the spine to move over from one side of a ramp to the other.

transitions (tran-SIH-shunz) The parts of a ramp that curve in a wavelike shape.

vertical (VER-tih-kul) In an up-and-down direction.

vert ramps (VERT RAMPS) The largest types of half-pipes, with walls that are completely vertical at the top. Most vert ramps are between 10 feet (3 m) and 13 feet (4 m) high.

Index

F
flat bars, 21–22
flat bottom, 5–6

G
Gonzales, Mark, 22
grind box(es), 17–18, 21. *See also* ledges.
grinds, 6, 13, 21

H
handrails, 14, 22

K
kick flips, 18

L
ledges, 14. *See also* grind boxes.

lip(s), 6, 13, 17

M
manuals, 17
mini ramp, 10

N
Northside Aztlan Community Center, 13

O
ollie, 17

P
pyramid(s), 18, 21

Q
Quarterly Skateboarder, The, 5

R
Riverside Skatepark, 10

S
Skatelab Skatepark, 10
spine(s), 13
street course(s), 14, 22
surfers, 5

T
transfer, 13
transitions, 6, 13

V
vert half-pipe, 14
vert ramps, 9–10

Y
YMCA Skatepark, 9

Web Sites

Due to the changing nature of Internet links, PowerKids Press has developed an online list of Web sites related to the subject of this book. This site is updated regularly. Please use this link to access the list: www.powerkidslinks.com/skate/ramps/

ML

10/06